ECSTASY: THE DANGER OF FALSE EUPHORIA

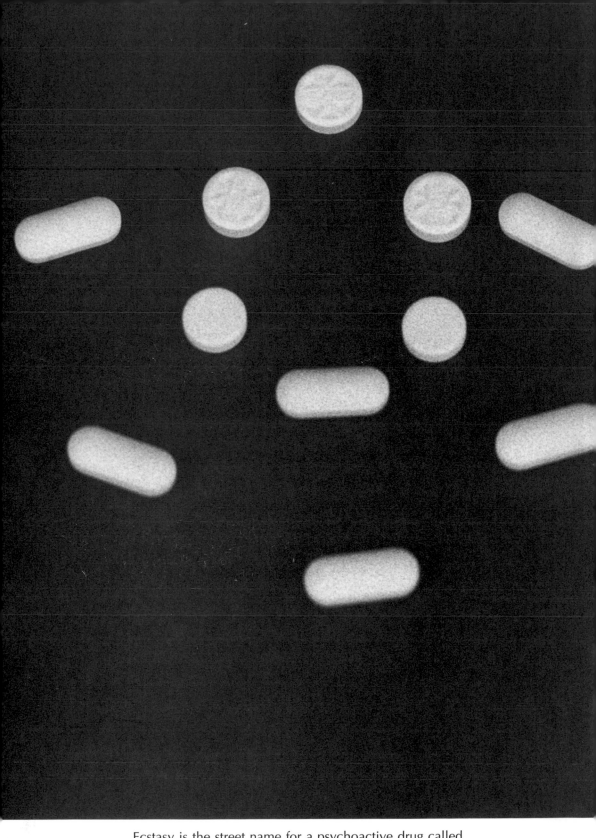

Ecstasy is the street name for a psychoactive drug called MDMA, which has become increasingly popular among teens. Ecstasy usually comes in the form of a tablet or capsule.

THE DRUG ABUSE PREVENTION LIBRARY

ECSTASY: THE DANGER OF FALSE EUPHORIA

Anne Alvergue

THE ROSEN PUBLISHING GROUP, INC.
NEW YORK

Published in 1998 by The Rosen Publishing Group, Inc.
29 East 21st Street, New York, NY 10010

First Edition

Library of Congress Cataloging-in-Publication Data

Alvergue, Anne.
     Ecstasy: the danger of false euphoria / Anne Alvergue.
          p.   cm. — (The drug abuse prevention library)
     Includes bibliographical references and index.
     Summary: Discusses the drug MDMA, commonly known as ecstasy, and its effects on the mind and body, particularly pointing out the dangers of using it.
     ISBN 0-8239-2506-4
     1. MDMA (Drug)—Juvenile literature.
2. Teenagers—Drug use—United States—Juvenile literature.   3. Drug abuse—United States—Prevention—Juvenile literature.   [1. MDMA (Drug).
2. Drug abuse.]   I. Title.   II. Series.
HV5822.M38A43   1997
362.29'9—dc21   97-8841
                                                           CIP
                                                           AC

Manufactured in the United States of America.

Contents

Introduction

*T*he popularity of the drug commonly known as Ecstasy is growing in youth culture. The Beastie Boys sing about it. Brandon from the TV show *Beverly Hills 90210* took it once at a dance club. You might even know someone who uses Ecstasy.

Although Ecstasy is not a new drug, it has recently become very popular among young people who go to nightclubs or to large dance parties called "raves." They like the way Ecstasy makes them feel: euphoric (happy and carefree), excited, and at ease with themselves and with others.

What teens may not realize is that
Ecstasy is an illegal drug that has a high

potential for abuse. It can have severe emotional and physical side effects. Some users have even died after using this drug.

If you are thinking about experimenting with Ecstasy, learn more about it before you make this important decision. Drug education can't hurt you, but drugs can. In this book we will discuss what Ecstasy is and how it affects you. We will explore the dangers involved in using Ecstasy. You will also learn about addiction and where you can turn for help if you have a drug abuse problem.

As a teen, it is easy to get confused about drugs because you hear a lot of conflicting messages. Your parents and teachers tell you to "just say no," but they might not explain the actual risks involved in taking drugs. Some of your peers might tell you that drugs are fun. Don't be misled by others. Get the facts yourself before you do something you might regret.

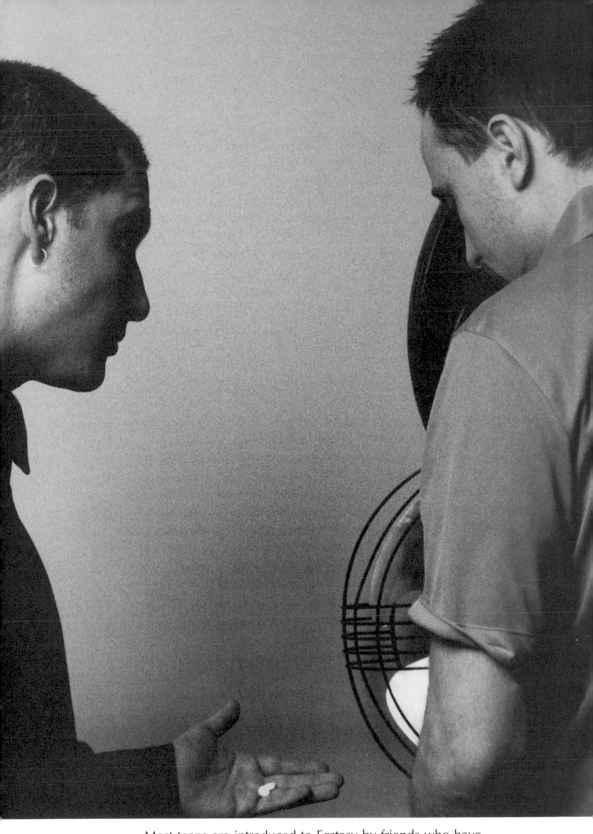

Most teens are introduced to Ecstasy by friends who have already tried it.

What Is Ecstasy?

Abby went to her first rave last summer. She had such a good time that she started going to raves every weekend. She made a lot of new friends. Some of them offered her a drug called Ecstasy. They told her that "X" would make her feel better than she had ever felt before—like she could do anything she wanted.

It seemed like almost everyone at raves did Ecstasy and had a good time. Abby felt left out and wanted to share the Ecstasy experience with her friends. One night, she decided to try X. She swallowed a pill that she bought through a friend and waited for the great feeling that everybody had told her she would experience.

9

10 | *After about half an hour, Abby began to feel a wave of energy go through her, like an adrenaline rush. That energy made her want to dance, talk to people, and touch things. She felt very confident. It was as if all her insecurities had slipped away. Everybody seemed so happy and friendly. Abby also became very sensitive to things she touched, saw, and heard. Colors seemed more vivid, and her body felt totally in synch with the music.*

Abby danced for hours until she became very hot and almost collapsed. She stumbled across the dance floor to find a water fountain. As Abby tried to weave through the crowd of dancers, she became disoriented by all the lights flashing into her eyes. The pounding music made her feel like her brain would explode. She became worried that everyone was staring at her.

Abby returned to the dance floor to find her friends. They hugged her when she rejoined them and urged her to continue dancing. Abby's friends were high on Ecstasy too, so they didn't realize that Abby was feeling sick and really needed help. Abby had to call her parents and ask them if they could come to pick her up. Once she got home safely, she felt very lonely and upset at herself for getting into this situation.

Many teens who take Ecstasy are not aware of the serious health risks that are involved.

What Abby took is a drug called MDMA (short for the chemical substance 3,4-methylenedioxy-methamphetamine). On the street, it is often called "Ecstasy," "X," "E," or "Adam."

Drugs are nonfood substances that people use to change the way their bodies normally work. Drugs include legal substances, like caffeine and aspirin, as well as illegal substances, like heroin and cocaine. For the most part, drugs that have accepted medical uses and no serious side effects are legal. (Alcohol and tobacco are notable exceptions.) On the other hand, drugs that have no accepted

Drugs are classified into different categories according to their effects. For example, Ecstasy, like marijuana, is considered a hallucinogen because it can cause users to see things differently than they appear.

medical value, or drugs that are very harmful or addictive, are usually illegal. MDMA is an illegal drug with no accepted medical use.

Some drugs come from natural sources, such as plants or mushrooms, while others are created artificially with chemicals. MDMA is a synthetic (human-made) drug created in laboratories.

Drugs are divided into different categories according to their effects and chemical makeup. For example, alcohol is a depressant, or "downer," because it slows down the normal activity of the body when consumed. Caffeine, on the other hand, is a stimulant, or "upper," because it speeds up the body's activities. Drugs that affect the mind or behavior are known as psychoactive drugs. Some psychoactive drugs cause users to see images or hear sounds that don't really exist. This sensory experience is called a hallucination. A drug that causes hallucinations is called a hallucinogen.

MDMA, or Ecstasy, is a psychoactive drug. It is classified as a hallucinogen because it can cause distortions in how you see things. It also acts like a group of stimulants called amphetamines. Like amphetamines, Ecstasy speeds up the way the body works.

Drugs also differ in the way they are taken and in how much they cost. Drugs can be snorted (inhaled through the nose), taken intravenously (injected through a vein directly into the bloodstream with a syringe), smoked, or taken orally (through the mouth). Ecstasy comes in the form of a tablet, capsule, or loose powder. It is usually taken orally, although it can be snorted, smoked, or injected as well. Each "hit" of Ecstasy

14 | generally costs between $20 and $35.

The History of Ecstasy

Although MDMA was developed more than eighty years ago, it was not widely used as a recreational drug until the 1980s.

A German chemical company called Merck first made MDMA in 1912. It was created as a diet pill, but there is no evidence that suggests that it was ever used or sold for this purpose.

In 1965, MDMA was recreated in the United States by a chemist named Alexander Shulgin. He shared his discovery with a small group of friends, including some psychiatrists.

During the 1970s, small groups of psychiatrists began experimenting with MDMA as an aid in psychotherapy (treatment of mental disorders). They believed that patients who took MDMA in a relaxed setting under a doctor's supervision could benefit from the drug by releasing their fears and enabling them to communicate freely. With the help of MDMA, patients could work through many of their problems. The doctors compared the drug's effects to Adam's innocent and blissful state in the biblical Garden of Eden, before he ate the forbidden fruit from the Tree of Knowledge. For this reason, they called the drug "Adam."

In the early 1980s, some small drug manufacturers learned of the euphoric feelings caused by MDMA and started producing the drug for recreational use. Some bars in Dallas and Fort Worth, Texas, began selling Ecstasy to yuppies and young adults and promoting "Ecstasy parties." Word about Ecstasy began to spread, and the demand and supply for the drug grew across the nation. At the time, MDMA was not yet a controlled substance under federal law and was, therefore, still legal.

The Controlled Substances Act of 1970 places all substances that are regulated by federal law into one of five schedules, or categories. Substances are classified according to their safety, medical uses, and potential for abuse. All drugs within the same schedule are subject to the same legal restrictions and penalties.

In June 1985, the Drug Enforcement Administration (DEA) banned MDMA and placed it in the most restrictive category of illegal drugs, Schedule I, which also

16 | includes heroin and LSD. Schedule I drugs are considered to have a high potential for abuse and no accepted medical use. It is illegal to make, possess, or sell any Schedule I drug in the United States.

The DEA reportedly classified MDMA as a Schedule I drug because researchers found that a chemically related drug, MDA, caused brain damage in rats. This led researchers to question whether MDA and related drugs like MDMA can cause damage in the human brain.

Ecstasy and the Rave Culture

Since the mid-1980s, Ecstasy has had a wide appeal among young people who are part of the rave culture. However, its use is not limited to this subculture—people from all walks of life have tried Ecstasy.

Raves are makeshift and usually illegal parties that take place in abandoned warehouses, parks, or nightclubs. They can last all night long. Raves are popular among teenagers and college students. They can be very large, with thousands of people in attendance.

Many raves are illegal because they are unlicensed. To be considered legal, a dance club must follow strict regulations and obtain various permits and licenses.

Ecstasy is not the only drug used by teens in raves, many teens combine it with other drugs, such as alcohol.

Unlicensed raves can be very unsafe. Often, too many people are crammed into a space that is not designed to hold so many bodies. There have been cases of unlicensed raves where the floors have caved in beneath the weight of hundreds of dancers. Fire safety regulations are also frequently ignored.

Those who organize raves constantly change locations to avoid being shut down. Details about where the next rave will be held usually spread by word of mouth or, sometimes, through the use of

18 | an information hot line. Large parties are also promoted through colorful flyers found at record stores, trendy clothing stores, and skate shops. In recent years, many raves have been held at legal night-clubs that offer special rave nights.

At raves, DJs spin house, techno, trance, and jungle music at up to 180 beats per minute. While each kind of music has a distinct sound, all share a hypnotic rhythm, synthesizer sounds, and a general use of samples. Samples are fragments of other people's recordings that are mixed into a new recording through the use of electronic equipment. Sometimes "Ecstasy lyrics" are layered into the music. For example, one popular dance song called "Energy Flash" whispers "Ecstasy" over and over again behind the beat of the music. In this atmosphere, filled with the throbbing intensity of techno music, dancers called "ravers" often turn to drugs like Ecstasy to get high and dance all night.

While Americans were using Ecstasy even before the rave culture developed in the United States, it is clear that the drug's popularity increased as raves spread across the country. Ecstasy and electronic music inspired the rave dance

culture. Together, the drug and the music **19**
help create a trance-like state for ravers.
Ecstasy became an important part of the
rave dance culture in much the same way
that LSD became associated with a lot of
the psychedelic music of the 1960s, and
speed became associated with punk rock.
However, it's important to remember that
many of the people who go to raves do
not take drugs. They get a natural high
from dancing to good music and socializ-
ing with friends.

Not all Ecstasy use happens at raves
and nightclubs. Some people take Ecstasy
with friends at someone's house or at
smaller parties. Taking Ecstasy in a
quieter, familiar setting may make you
feel safer, but the effects of the drug don't
change. You still run the risk of suffering
serious consequences.

In 1995, a British teenager named
Leah Betts fell into a coma after taking
Ecstasy at her eighteenth birthday party
while her parents were home. She reportedly drank too much water to make up
for the dehydrating effects of Ecstasy.
Her body was unable to eliminate
enough water through sweating or urinating. She died when her body filled up
with excess fluid.

Ecstasy affects each person differently. There is no way to predict how your body will react to this drug.

Can You Be Sure It's Ecstasy?

Cameron first heard about Ecstasy from his older brother, Chris, who had taken it before and said it was fun. Cameron asked his brother if he could "score" some for him and his friends to try. Cameron figured, "If my brother has done it, I can do it too."

Chris gave his brother some Ecstasy. Cameron planned to take it at home with his friends on Friday night, when his parents were out of town. One of his friends, Andrew, was very scared—he had never taken a drug before and didn't know what to expect. He didn't want to try Ecstasy, but he didn't want to feel left out either.

Cameron and his friends swallowed the brown-speckled pills. After forty-five minutes, the teens started to feel the drug's effects. Cameron started to vomit and couldn't stop. His friend Jimmy became very drowsy and felt like he was going to faint. Andrew began to panic.

Nobody knew what to do. They all felt really sick. Cameron tried to call his parents, but he couldn't reach them. Luckily, his brother was in his college dorm. As soon as Chris heard what had happened, he rushed over. He was shocked to see how sick everyone was. Chris calmed them down by telling them the sickness would eventually pass. He gave them some cool water to drink and told them to lie down and try to relax.

Chris later found out that the brown-speckled pills he had given his brother probably contained heroin. He felt responsible for getting Cameron and his brother's friends into this horrible situation. He didn't know that Ecstasy pills could contain other drugs.

MDMA, or Ecstasy, is an illegal substance made in underground (secret) laboratories. This means that you can never be certain about its purity or dosage because

22 | you don't know who made it, what was put into it, or how much of the drug was used. Compare this to a legal drug like cold medicine, where you know the company that made a certain product, its ingredients, and potential side effects. Producers of legal drugs must meet strict government quality standards to ensure that their products are pure. On the other hand, those who make illegal drugs like MDMA are not subject to such controls.

As a result, much of the Ecstasy sold on the street is not pure MDMA. It is often "cut," or mixed, with contaminants (other substances) by the dealers who sell it in order to increase their profits. Contaminants may include cold medicine ingredients, harmless fillers, or even poisons. Other illegal drugs, like speed, heroin, or LSD, are sometimes found in Ecstasy tablets. These substances may produce undesired or unexpected effects that can seriously harm you. You can never be sure of what you are taking when you buy Ecstasy.

A Word on Herbal Ecstasy

Since Ecstasy became a popular recreational drug, some companies began marketing herbal look-alikes to teens.

With psychedelic packaging and promises of "a floaty, mind-expanding euphoria," products like "Herbal Ecstacy" have drawn teens who want to experience a legal and natural high.

Herbal ecstasy was created as a natural alternative to an illegal drug. It should not, however, be mistaken for MDMA. Herbal ecstasy is not made with the same ingredients as MDMA, nor does it produce the same high. The main ingredient in herbal ecstasy, ephedra, is a natural stimulant. It raises your blood pressure and heart rate and makes your skin tingle, but it doesn't affect the brain chemistry in the same way that MDMA does.

It is important to bear in mind that natural and legal don't necessarily mean safe. In large doses, herbal alternatives to Ecstasy can cause severe side effects. Ephedra has been linked to heart attacks, seizures, and death. The Food and Drug Administration (FDA) has issued a health warning about ephedra, and several states have declared it illegal to sell ephedra products as "mood-altering substances." However, the sale of ephedra products sold for other purposes, such as weight loss or bodybuilding, remains legal.

CHAPTER 2

How Does Ecstasy Affect You?

*A*udra had never tried Ecstasy until she went to a rave called "Lucky Charms." She didn't know anyone there except the one friend who had invited her. She was surrounded by boys in baggy clothes and girls with shiny suits and small backpacks. Audra felt out of place in her ordinary jeans and sweater.

A cute boy approached Audra and introduced himself. His name was Peter. "Do you want to have fun tonight?" he asked. "Sure," she answered. Peter led her into the bathroom, where he pulled out some white tablets from his pocket. He said everyone was doing it—didn't she want to join in the fun? Audra

24 | was attracted to Peter and didn't want him

Ecstasy changes the chemicals in your brain to produce feelings of euphoria. Users often report feeling confident and more outgoing.

to think she was uncool. She took the pill with some orange juice.

Within an hour, Audra was overwhelmed by an intense high. She wanted to move around and touch everything. She had never had so much confidence and ease in talking to people. She danced with Peter all night.

Now Audra goes to raves whenever she can so she can see Peter, get high, and dance. Ever since she started taking Ecstasy regularly, Audra has had difficulty concentrating in her classes. She often skips school to hang out with Peter and shop for CDs and clothes.

26 | *Lately, it has been hard for her to feel happy without getting high on Ecstasy.*

Facts About Ecstasy

A national survey found that in 1992, only 46 percent of the young adults surveyed in the nineteen- to twenty-two-year-old age group thought that trying MDMA put them at great risk for harming themselves. In 1995, 34 percent of the twelfth graders surveyed said that MDMA was "fairly easy" or "very easy" to get.

Much like rave locations, most young people get information about Ecstasy by word of mouth. In this way, they learn where to buy it, what its effects are, and whether it can hurt them.

All kinds of rumors about Ecstasy have spread. Some people claim that Ecstasy taps your spinal fluid and can permanently paralyze you. Others say that Ecstasy has no negative side effects. Both of these rumors are false. The rest of this chapter will sort out the facts from the myths about how Ecstasy can affect you.

How Ecstasy Affects the Body

Ecstasy affects the body's central nervous system—the brain and the spinal cord.

Once swallowed, Ecstasy enters the bloodstream and is carried throughout the body. Some reaches the brain, and some is broken down by the liver. Once inside the brain, Ecstasy increases the circulation of a substance called serotonin.

Serotonin is one of several substances in the brain that regulates your mood and how you feel. It is believed to trigger feelings of love and excitement.

The high that Ecstasy produces is the result of the brain being flooded with "feel-good" serotonin. Ecstasy forces the brain to change moods and maintain the high feeling for about four hours. During this time, Ecstasy prevents the brain from calming down by blocking the return and storage of serotonin. Normally, serotonin is released for immediate use and then stored for future use.

When the brain is drained of serotonin, the good feeling fades and users "crash." They feel tired, depressed, and unable to focus. These symptoms can last for days and sometimes even weeks.

Set and Setting

Ecstasy is a psychoactive drug. Psychoactive drugs usually make the user's mood or feelings more intense. A user's mood

When an Ecstasy high wears off, users often feel very tired and depressed.

may depend on the "set and setting" of the drug experience.

The "set" refers to your mind-set or what you are feeling and thinking at the time of your drug experience. If you are nervous and worried before taking Ecstasy, you will probably feel anxious while you're on it. The "setting" is where you are and who you are with. Taking Ecstasy with close friends at home will likely produce a different experience than taking it at a crowded dance party.

What Does an Ecstasy High Feel Like?

Users typically begin to feel the effects of a moderate dose of Ecstasy (75–100 mg) twenty to sixty minutes after swallowing it. The high lasts about four hours.

Some users experience unpleasant physical symptoms, which may include dryness of the mouth, jaw-clenching, faintness, chills, sweating, muscle tension, nausea or vomiting, dilated pupils, and blurred vision. Ecstasy also increases the heart rate, blood pressure, and body temperature.

MDMA takes its popular street name from the word "ecstasy"—a state of intense emotion. That is because users experience an initial rush of euphoria and

30 become very energetic and confident. This rush is followed by calmness and an absence of worry or anger. These feelings generally last two to three hours.

Some users say that Ecstasy makes them more expressive and outgoing. They may talk and smile a lot or want to hug people around them.

Ecstasy also changes the way you perceive things. Users often report heightened senses of touch, hearing, vision, taste, and smell. For example, simple actions, like running your fingers through your hair, may feel intensely pleasurable and new. Colors and sounds may seem clearer.

Raves—with their nonstop music, light and video shows, and hundreds of dancers—lend themselves to the Ecstasy experience because they indulge the senses and satisfy a user's desire to feel close to others.

CHAPTER 3

The Dangers of Ecstasy

*E*cstasy is not a risk-free drug. While it can give the user an intense high, it can also cause dangerous side effects and "bad trips."

Physical and Psychological Dangers

Not all teens feel good after taking Ecstasy. Some feel very anxious, confused, or paranoid while on the drug. They may even have a panic attack—a feeling of overwhelming fear with symptoms, such as nausea, hyperventilation, sweating, and rapid heartbeat. Such attacks can be dangerous because people rarely think clearly or use good judgment when they are so scared.

31

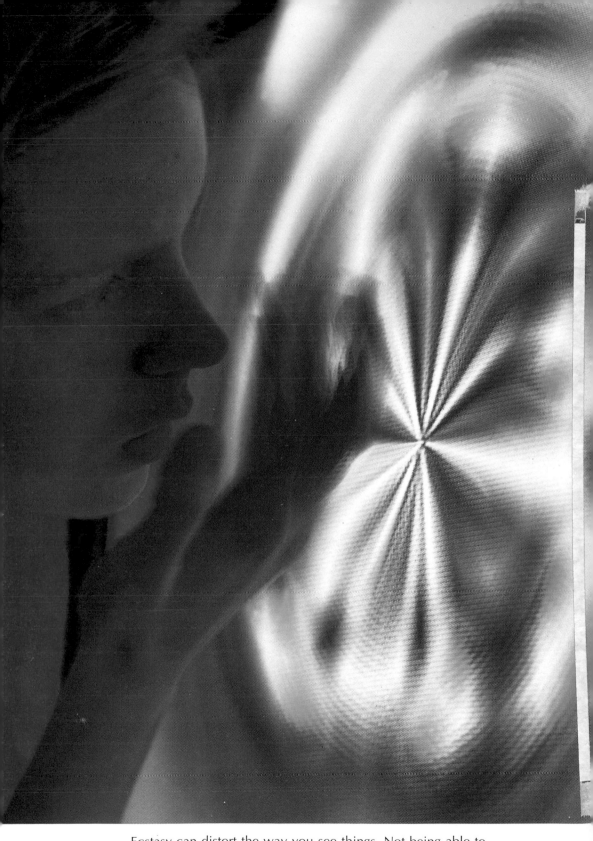

Ecstasy can distort the way you see things. Not being able to
see objects clearly may affect your coordination.

Teens who are angry or upset before using Ecstasy may become moody or violent when they are high because Ecstasy tends to exaggerate the user's mood.

Ecstasy can trick your mind into seeing objects differently than they appear. You may "see" trails of blurred images or objects vibrating when the objects are, in fact, still. This distortion can affect your judgment and coordination and lead to serious injury. For example, a person who is dancing on a stage while on Ecstasy may become so wrapped up in the flashing of the surrounding lights that he or she may fall off the stage.

Ecstasy increases your chances of worsening an injury because it decreases your sensitivity to pain. You might hurt yourself while you're high and not even know it until the effects of the drug wear off.

When users come down from an Ecstasy high, they often experience body chills. Some people have trouble walking after taking large doses of Ecstasy; they feel like they can't move their legs. Hours later, they may suffer pain in their lower back, joints, and muscles. Some people become irritable when coming off of Ecstasy. Many have trouble falling asleep.

Regular Ecstasy users may become very depressed and irritable when they are not high, which may lead to violence.

They may feel very tired the next day and eat very little. It is not unusual to feel listless and depressed for days.

Some people feel the side effects of Ecstasy even weeks after use. They may suffer from depression, anxiety, and even paranoia. Those who already suffer from depression may have long-term anxiety disorders that make them feel nervous all the time.

In rare cases, frequent users have suffered long-term consequences, including liver and kidney damage and psychosis—a mental condition in which a person loses touch with reality.

The Dangers of Mixing Ecstasy with Other Drugs

A further danger involved in using Ecstasy is not knowing exactly what you are taking or how strong it is. Ecstasy is frequently mixed with other drugs or substances that can cause unpredictable reactions. For example, taking Ecstasy that is "laced" with LSD may cause you to hallucinate for up to twelve hours. This "trip" can be very scary and dangerous if you are not expecting it.

You also don't know how strong an Ecstasy pill will be. Very high doses of

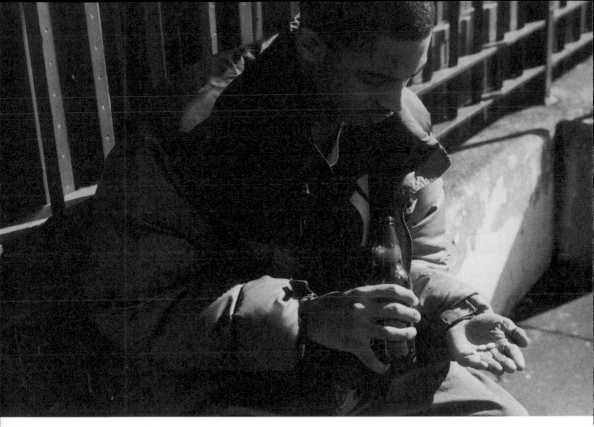

Mixing Ecstasy with other drugs can be hazardous to your health. For example, the combination of alcohol and Ecstasy may cause users to become dangerously dehydrated.

Ecstasy cause the user to be more alert and excited than euphoric. This may result in a dissatisfying or dangerous high.

The only way to be sure of what is in an Ecstasy pill is to have it tested. Some nightclubs in the Netherlands have Ecstasy testing booths that analyze tablets for contaminants. In the United States, such testing is not available. The bottom line is that you never know what you are getting when you take Ecstasy.

Some young people who experiment with Ecstasy intentionally mix different drugs to get higher during their trip or to come down easier. This can be very dangerous for many reasons.

For example, mixing Ecstasy with an amphetamine—a drug often used by ravers to feel more energetic—greatly increases your risk of overheating, particularly in a crowded party setting where you are likely to lose fluids by sweating. Drinking alcohol when you are high on Ecstasy is dangerous because both drugs cause dehydration and put a lot of stress on your liver. People who take antidepressants should also avoid taking Ecstasy because the combination can cause dangerously high blood pressure.

Casualties from Ecstasy Use

Little is known about Ecstasy's long-term effects on the human body and mind. This is partly because it has only recently become popular as a recreational drug. And since it is an illegal drug, the government has allowed limited research on the effects of MDMA in humans. Government-approved studies are currently under way to determine whether MDMA causes brain damage and other long-term health hazards. What *is* known is that young people have suffered complications after taking Ecstasy, and some have died.

Overdosing on Ecstasy, or taking too much of the drug for your body to handle, can cause you to vomit continuously, hyperventilate, or pass out. If you have a pre-existing health condition, such as heart, liver, or kidney problems, or if you suffer from asthma, epilepsy, diabetes, or depression, taking Ecstasy is a particularly serious health risk. But even young people in good health have suffered permanent damage after taking Ecstasy.

One of the most common reasons for complications or death associated with Ecstasy use is overheating or heatstroke. Heatstroke occurs when the body's internal thermometer fails, and the body is exposed to excessive heat.

Your body is usually able to maintain a stable internal temperature even when it is very hot outside. If your body temperature rises, your body sweats to cool off. But when you are exposed to high temperatures for a long time, your body may not be able to cool off sufficiently. In extreme cases, heatstroke can lead to seizure, coma, or death.

Several incidents of heatstroke have been linked to Ecstasy use at raves. Research suggests that Ecstasy itself increases body temperature and can cause dehydration. The stimulant effect of Ecstasy can also contribute, indirectly, to causing heatstroke. That is because Ecstasy enables users to dance longer than they normally would without feeling tired. They often dance for hours in a hot and crowded area without taking a break to cool down or replenish the fluids they've lost from sweating.

Ecstasy tends to hide your sense of thirst even when your body is being drained of fluids as you sweat. Since Ecstasy can mask the danger signals of overheating, victims may not even try to cool down or drink when they are hot and dehydrated.

Danger signs of heatstroke include an abnormally high body temperature (about 105 degrees), rapid heartbeat, quick and shallow breathing, and abnormally high or low blood pressure. Faintness, confusion, and panic attacks can also occur.

If you detect a danger sign of heatstroke, you should retreat immediately to an area that is quiet and cool. Sit or lay down. Rest and drink fluids like water or fruit juice. Let friends or someone you can trust know about your condition so that they can seek emergency medical

40 | help, if necessary. You should be treated with cool compresses and fanned as you wait for help to arrive.

In some cases, death has resulted from drinking *too much* water. Drinking more fluids than your body can get rid of can cause kidney failure and other complications. Drinking lots of water and not urinating is a dangerous sign that your body is not functioning properly. Seek emergency medical help if you detect this danger sign.

Social Dangers

Teens who use Ecstasy think they are on top of the world and can do anything. This attitude can lead to unreasonable and dangerous behavior. For example, you may want to drive your car even though you are high. This kind of poor judgment can get you into a serious accident.

Ecstasy tends to make people feel more emotional and sensual. Some users express affection toward strangers, which may be misinterpreted and taken advantage of. Users may become more open to physical intimacy than they normally would be. They may make decisions that they might regret. It's easy to forget about

Ecstasy may make some users feel more sensual. When teens are high, they may use poor judgment and have unprotected sex, leading to pregnancy or sexually transmitted diseases.

protected sex when you're high. But it won't be so easy to forget about an unwanted pregnancy or a sexually transmitted disease (STD) if you catch one. It only takes one unprotected sexual encounter to get pregnant or to contract HIV, the virus that causes the incurable disease called AIDS.

Legal Dangers
Getting involved with Ecstasy can get you into trouble with the law. Driving under the influence (DUI) and possessing or

42 | selling an illegal drug can take you straight to jail. If you are a minor and are caught with Ecstasy, you will likely be sent to a juvenile detention center and may be sentenced to a one-year probation. If you are over eighteen years old, you may be sent to prison for up to five years.

Ecstasy is an expensive drug. Most teens cannot afford to use it regularly. Some teens have resorted to stealing from family and friends or robbing strangers to get money to buy Ecstasy.

Frequent users sometimes buy Ecstasy in quantities of ten hits or more. They then resell the Ecstasy at a higher price to cover the costs of their own doses. Whether you buy ten hits to share with your friends or to sell to strangers, you are considered a drug dealer in the eyes of the law and will be prosecuted accordingly.

CHAPTER 4

Addiction

*W*hen a drug user feels an intense desire to use a drug that is known to be harmful and continues to give into the craving, he or she may become addicted. If the user satisfies this craving frequently, he or she can quickly build up a tolerance to the drug, needing more each time to achieve the same effect. This occurs because the body becomes less responsive to the effects of a drug after repeated use. A user may feel the need to use a drug even if it no longer produces any sense of pleasure. An addict sometimes suffers painful physical and psychological symptoms, or withdrawal symptoms, that occur when he or she stops taking the drug.

44   The levels of addiction differ from drug to drug. Some drugs, like heroin and alcohol, are physically addictive. This means that an addict's body *needs* the drug on a regular basis; otherwise he or she will suffer withdrawal symptoms, such as nausea or stomach cramps.

Other drugs, like Ecstasy, can be psychologically addictive. This means that users feel the need to use a drug to feel good, but they won't necessarily suffer physical withdrawal symptoms without it. They may, however, suffer psychological withdrawal symptoms, such as severe depression and anxiety. Psychological dependence on a drug may be more subtle than physical addiction, but it isn't any less serious.

Generally, a person's first experience with Ecstasy is the strongest. Continued use over a long period of time brings diminishing returns, or fewer positive and more negative effects. Tolerance develops to Ecstasy's euphoric effects, and the drug begins to feel more like a "speed rush." Because the user doesn't feel the same high over time, Ecstasy is less likely to be abused for very long periods than most other "hard" drugs.

Teens who start experimenting with alcohol and cigarettes for fun may move on to harder drugs like Ecstasy to experience a more intense high.

How Do You Become Addicted?

The road to drug addiction usually starts with experimental use, when teens first try drugs. Most start experimenting with alcohol, cigarettes, or marijuana. If they like the experience, they may eventually move on to harder drugs to get a more intense high. Repeated use of a habit-forming drug can easily develop into addiction.

Some users get trapped in a cycle of drug dependency by becoming part of a social scene that involves drugs. For example, teens who go to raves often

46 experiment with Ecstasy because drugs are part of the scene. Sometimes, dealers give free Ecstasy to first-time users to hook them on the drug. Some teens feel great the first time they use Ecstasy, so they try it again. Many find that their high isn't quite the same the second time, so they try Ecstasy over and over again in an attempt to recapture their first experience with the drug.

"Binge users" take from three to ten hits of Ecstasy at a time. Often, they "boost" or "stack" their dosage by taking more hits throughout the trip to lengthen their high. However, taking multiple or repeated doses of Ecstasy usually increases the stimulant effect, not the euphoria. By not allowing the body to go through its normal mood cycles, the user will eventually crash and feel so depressed that he or she will want to do more of the drug.

Depression is one of the side effects of Ecstasy use, and users often depend on Ecstasy to bring them out of their depression. But many users find that the more they use Ecstasy the more they become depressed when they are not high. Although they feel miserable much of the time, they can't bring themselves to stop

Using Ecstasy regularly can make it hard to stay focused at school.

using Ecstasy because it brings temporary relief to their depression. They become caught in a no-win situation.

Ray started taking Ecstasy six months ago, when he went to his first rave. Now that Ray is in the scene, he goes out every chance he gets—to "full moon raves," "Mushroom Mondays," and weekend all-nighters. He takes a lot of X, the drug of choice at parties, but he doesn't get as high as he used to. So he boosts his high by taking more X.

Ray is failing his classes. When he goes to school, he can't concentrate. It's hard for him to sit still. He thinks everyone is staring at him.

48 | *One day, Ray snapped at one of his friends in class because he thought his friend was giving him a funny look. When Ray's friend told him that he was being paranoid, Ray pushed him to the ground and started hitting him. The principal suspended Ray.*

After being suspended, Ray began to realize that drugs were taking control of his life and that he needed help. He went to see the school's drug counselor because he wanted to get his life back on track.

How Addiction Can Affect Your Life

Drug addiction dominates your life. It takes your attention away from important social activities, including school, work, and spending time with family and friends. If you are an addict, you will continue to use drugs even if you hurt yourself or those around you. Repeated use of Ecstasy can wreak havoc on your health, social life, mental ability, and sense of well-being.

CHAPTER 5

Why Teens Use Drugs

*B*eing a teen means changing, trying new things, and deciding what you like to do. This is the time that you begin to develop your identity. You want to act like an adult and make your own decisions. Some teens experiment with drugs during this time of change to feel independent and explore new feelings.

Most teens who try drugs for the first time are curious. They want to know what will happen, how they will feel, or what they will see. Curiosity is a natural feeling. It is very dangerous, though, to use a drug you don't know anything about, just because you are curious.

Some teens use drugs to cope with the pressures of adolescence. For example, it

50 | is common in school to want to fit in and do what everyone else is doing. Others around you may be experimenting with drugs. This may seem like an easy way to look cool or feel like part of the "in" crowd.

As a teenager, you may feel very insecure, especially about the way you look because your body is changing so much. You may take drugs to forget your anxieties and to feel more confident.

Drugs are often used as a way to cope with, or block out, problems. Some teens have trouble at home or at school and feel like they have no one to turn to for help. They may take drugs to feel better. After the high wears off, though, they often feel worse than they did before. Taking drugs doesn't make your problems disappear; it only creates more problems.

Some teens think that drug use is acceptable because they see their parents or siblings abusing drugs. Their attitudes toward drugs may also be influenced by the media—magazines, television, and movies—which sometimes glamorize drugs. Seeing a favorite actor using drugs in a movie may lead you to think that drugs are okay.

Teens turn to drugs like Ecstasy for many different reasons: to feel happy, to feel more secure in social settings, or to forget their problems. Yet Ecstasy and other drugs only offer a temporary and artificial sense of control, confidence, and happiness. Lasting happiness can't come from a drug.

A Self-test for Teens

How are drugs affecting your life? If you think you or a friend may have a drug problem, take the following self-test for teens from the National Council on Alcoholism and Drug Dependence.

- Do you use drugs to build self-confidence?
- Do you ever drink or get high immediately after you have a problem at home or at school?
- Have you ever missed school due to drugs?
- Does it bother you if someone says that you use too much alcohol or other drugs?
- Have you started hanging out with a heavy-drinking or drug-using crowd?
- Are drugs affecting your reputation?
- Do you borrow money or "do without" other things to buy drugs?

52

- Do you feel guilty after using drugs?
- Do you feel a sense of power when you use drugs?
- Do you use drugs until your supply is gone?
- Have you lost friends since you started using drugs?
- Do you feel more at ease in social situations when using drugs?
- Have you ever been arrested or hospitalized due to use of alcohol or illegal drugs?
- Has anyone in your family had drinking or other drug problems?
- Do you ever wake up and wonder what happened the night before?

If you answered yes to several of these questions, you may have a drug problem. Read on to find information about getting help.

CHAPTER 6

Help for Teens

If drugs are interfering with school and your relationships with family and friends, and if you just can't say no even when you want to, your drug use may be turning into an addiction. Seek help today before it's too late.

If you phone an organization or hot line number, you will speak to a trained counselor. You don't have to tell the counselor who you are, and he or she won't tell on you or force you to stop. If you are hesitant to talk openly about your problems, just ask some general questions, like "How do you know if you have a drug problem?" or "I have a friend who may have a problem with Ecstasy; how

There is help available to teens who have a drug abuse problem. By calling a drug abuse organization or hot line, you can speak to a trained counselor who will help you.

can I help?" The counselor will listen to you, answer your questions, and advise you on the best possible solutions to your problem.

It is best to talk to someone in person about your concerns. If you don't feel comfortable approaching your parents, consider speaking to a friend, a school counselor, a sports coach, or a student aide.

You may be referred to a local out-reach treatment clinic where you can talk to a drug counselor for free or at a low cost. There are clinics just for teens, too.

After Ray was kicked out of school, he realized he had two choices. He could continue doing drugs. Or he could stop, go back to school, and pursue his goals.

Even though Ray was addicted, he was tired of the same old routine: get high, feel miserable when the X wears off, and then get high again. He felt like his life was going nowhere. He wanted to go back to school and take more art classes. He remembered his teacher telling him that he was very good at drawing.

Ray's school counselor referred him to a local outreach center. Although Ray was very nervous and scared, the counselor at the

You can begin the road to recovery from drug abuse by speaking to a trusted adult, such as a school counselor or family relative.

center was very understanding and made him feel better. She didn't make him feel guilty for his past. She encouraged him to take part in a support group for teen drug abusers at the center.

It was hard, at first, to stop doing drugs. But it helped to talk out his frustrations with the other teens in his support group. He made new friends and didn't feel like he had to go back to the old social scene.

When you enter a clinic, you will meet with a counselor one-on-one. The counselor will want to develop an open relationship with you to help you get better. He or she may ask what the drug is doing for you and explain how your drug use has turned to abuse. You will also receive drug education.

Next, you may join a support group where you share your drug abuse experiences with other drug users. This support group may be available at an outreach clinic or at a self-help group like Narcotics Anonymous. It may be hard, at first, to talk openly. But once you admit to having a drug abuse problem, you will have taken an important step toward your recovery. You are accepting your mistakes and getting on with your life. You don't have to feel alone anymore because others in your group know how you feel. They will support you through your recovery.

If your drug abuse problem is very serious, you may require inpatient treatment. This is a long-term recovery program: The addict lives in a special treatment center until he or she overcomes addiction. Getting over a drug problem will be challenging, but you will become a stronger and happier person for it.

58 *Ray is now back in school. He is in a drawing class and wants to become a cartoonist. He has already started his own fanzine, and it has received a great response from his friends and teachers. Everyone seems really impressed by his talent and initiative. Ray is so busy with his fanzine that he has little time to think about drugs.*

Ray hopes to publish his own comic book someday. He knows that doing drugs isn't going to help him reach his goal.

Like Ray, you may realize that you don't need to use drugs to feel good about yourself or to have a good time. In fact, drugs often prevent you from excelling in what you like to do. Developing a creative interest or hobby—whether it is drawing, dancing, playing basketball, or starting your own band—will help you find more fulfilling ways to spend your time than getting high.

Glossary—*Explaining New Words*

addiction A condition in which a person intensely craves a drug and is unable to stop using it despite the harm it causes.

amphetamine A stimulant drug that speeds up the activities of the body.

anxiety Feeling of fear or unease usually caused by a situation that one feels unable to cope with.

contaminants Impurities or fillers added to a pure substance.

dehydration Loss of body fluids or water.

depression State of sadness marked by feelings of hopelessness and withdrawal from daily activities.

diminishing returns A decrease in the pleasurable effects of a drug caused by the tolerance developed through regular use.

drug A nonfood substance that affects your mind and body.

ecstasy A state of sudden and intense emotion.

euphoria A feeling of happiness and well-being.

hallucination A sensory experience in which a person sees or hears things that don't really exist.

60   **hallucinogen**   A substance that causes hallucinations.

heatstroke   Condition in which the body's thermometer breaks down, and the body is overexposed to heat.

hyperventilate   To breathe abnormally, rapidly and deeply.

overdose   An excessive amount of a drug that can cause severe damage or death.

physical   Having to do with the body.

psychoactive drug   Drug that affects one's mood and behavior.

psychological   Having to do with the mind.

rave   Large dance party with techno music and light and video shows.

serotonin   A brain chemical that is believed to regulate one's mood.

synthetic   Made from a chemical process. Not made naturally.

techno music   A style of disco music heard at raves and nightclubs. It consists of fast synthesizer rhythms and sampled music.

tolerance   Resistance to a drug's effects gained through continuous use.

withdrawal symptoms   Painful physical or psychological symptoms that occur when a person stops using an addictive drug.

Where to Go for Help

Associations

Nar-Anon Family
World Service Office
(310) 547-5800
For relatives and friends
of drug abusers

National Clearinghouse
for Alcohol and Drug
Information
P.O. Box 2345
Rockville, MD 20847-
2345
(800) 729-6686
Web site: http://www.
health.org

National Council on
Alcoholism & Drug
Dependence
12 West 21st Street
New York, NY 10010
(800) 622-2255

Support Groups and Referral Hot Lines

Mental Health Crisis
Line
(800) 222-8220

Narcotics Anonymous
P.O. Box 9999
Van Nuys, CA 94109
(818) 773-9999

National Drug and
Alcohol Referral Line
(800) 821-4357

The National Institute of
Drug Abuse (NIDA)
(800) 662-HELP

National Youth Crisis Hot
Line
(800) 448-4663

Tough Love
(800) 333-1069

IN CANADA

Alcohol and Drug
Dependency Informa-
tion and Counseling
Services
2471 1/2 Portage Avenue,
#2
Winnipeg, MB R3J 0N6
(204) 831-1999

Narcotics Anonymous
P.O. Box 7500, Station A
Toronto, ON M5W 1P9
(416) 691-9519

For Further Reading

Berger, Gilda. *Make Up Your Mind About Drugs*. New York: E. P. Dutton, 1988.

Cohen, Susan, and Daniel Cohen. *What You Can Believe About Drugs*. New York: M. Evans and Company, Inc., 1987.

O'Donnell Rawls, Bea, and Gwen Johnson. *Drugs and Where to Turn*. New York: The Rosen Publishing Group, Inc., 1993

Robbins, Paul R. *Designer Drugs*. Springfield, NJ: Enslow Publishers, 1995.

Weil, Andrew, and Winifred Rosen. *Chocolate to Morphine: Everything You Need to Know About Mind-Altering Drugs*. Boston: Houghton Mifflin, 1993.

Index

About the Author

Anne Alvergue is a freelance writer and video editor/producer. She has taught in middle schools and at the college level, while attending U.C. Berkeley.

    Ms. Alvergue lives in San Francisco.

Photo Credits

Cover by Michael Brandt; all other photos by Seth Dinnerman.